Kirkmichael, in the ~~~

The simple grey headstone that marks w~
Duncan, the author) is buried stands on the
Kirkmichael. Just over the wall, the waters o
Across the Bay from Kirkmichael lies Jemima
Jane Duncan lived the latter part of her life, Rc   ~.. ~tore. High
above Jemimaville lies the hillside croft of ~.. ~oiony, where she spent her
formative childhood holidays.

This booklet, produced to raise funds for the Kirkmichael Trust, which seeks to restore the derelict Kirkmichael building to a beneficial community and visitor resource, provides a guide to the Colony and Jemimaville. Jane Duncan regarded this area as her *"home place"*, her moral reference point and a creative inspiration. The history of Jemimaville, the Colony and the Cameron family is included.

This guide to the area complements the booklet *"Jane Duncan"* which celebrates the life and work of Jane Duncan and is published by Millrace Publishing in 2010, the centenary of her birth. Additional material and photography on Jemimaville may be found in *"Resolis 'Slope of Light' Guide to a Black Isle Parish"* (2009), available for purchase from the Kirkmichael Trust website www.kirkmichael.info.

I am indebted to the Cameron family; Kenny and Joy Foubister, the owners of the Old Store; Andrew Dowsett, Scoulag (cover photography); Cromarty Courthouse; Hugh Scott, Jemimaville and Douglas Matheson, Cromarty, for photographs or information. All modern photography, unless otherwise indicated, is by the author.

Above: Artist's impression of the Kirkmichael restoration *(artwork Mike Taylor)*
Left: Gravestone of Elizabeth Jane Cameron (Jane Duncan), 1910-1976 *(photography Andrew Dowsett)*

The Colony

At a height of 500 feet above Jemimaville, on an exposed hillside buffeted by the winds from Ben Wyvis, lies the crofting area of the Colony. The village and the croft are hidden from each other by the steep braeface.

In her fiction, Jane Duncan returned time and again to *"Reachfar"* as a kind of spiritual touching base. Much of the fictional physical environment has its factual equivalent on the ground.

Thus, in *"My Friend Monica"* she describes her special *"Thinking Place"*, a quiet spot in the fir trees on the moor *"About a quarter of a mile from the house, above the spring-fed well which supplies our water"*. Take a look at a detailed map (the ground is now too overgrown to explore) and there's the well above the house, with the fir trees on the moor beyond it.

Another example. She observes in the old quarry at Reachfar an early and very disturbing incident in *"My Friends the Miss Boyds"*. This old quarry lay *"at the south-easternmost corner of Reachfar"*. On the ground we can still see the defile which, on early Ordnance Survey mapping, is revealed to be a substantial quarry, although not of the commercial significance she portrays.

And, of course, the wider environment is exactly the same. The snow-touched bulk of Ben Wyvis, the ships of the Fleet lying in the Firth, the morning mail train to Wick *"running along the north shore of the Firth like a little black caterpillar"*, the farmcarts going down to the coal-boat coming into Cromarty (*"Achcraggan"* was a fusion of Cromarty and Jemimaville), were all there in reality. Her social descriptions, as in croft life or the division of the fisher-town from the remainder of Cromarty, were based on sharp observation.

Like most homes in the area, built before modern windtight construction allowed residents to appreciate the view to the Firth, it is turned from the prevailing cold winds from the north west. Instead, its windows and doors open to the sunshine of the south, and the buildings provide shelter for garden and yard. The view and significance of the single back window (from which night-time visitors coming up the hill could see the light of a guiding candle) are splendidly set out by a young Jane Duncan in an extract of an unpublished novel included within the commemorative booklet "*Jane Duncan*": "*From October till March, the north wind makes attack after attack, sweeping down over the hills, across the surly Firth, and flinging itself against the house and the Back Window...*"

Right: View through the Back Window

Opposing page: The Colony in 2010

The croft lies just within the Parish of Cromarty, so far out that its neighbour, Upperwood Croft, lies in the Parish of Resolis. Access was via the farm track (just a trace of which now occurs on the ground) to the Ardeville road and then down to the main Cromarty road. A track also ran more directly east to Peddieston.

The Colony lay on the extremities of the Cromarty Estate though baptism registry entries in the 1840s call it "*the Colony, Udale*". Poyntzfield and Udale Estates (Jane Duncan's "*Poyntdale*") are to the north west and north respectively. On the origin of the name, "*Letter from Reachfar*" states: "*It was called 'The Colony' I have been told because once upon a time a colony of weavers lived on that ground, who gradually died off and drifted away, leaving mine as the last surviving family who gradually took over the abandoned sixty acres of marginal arable and the hundred and fifty of moorland.*" Whilst I note "*Shuttletown*", suggestive of weaving, lay about this location, not one of the 56 residents of the Colony in 1841 was a weaver. But then, the combined evidence of 1841 and 1851 Census returns is that most of the heads of households in the Colony at that period had moved into the Parish relatively recently, suggesting the original tenants had moved on.

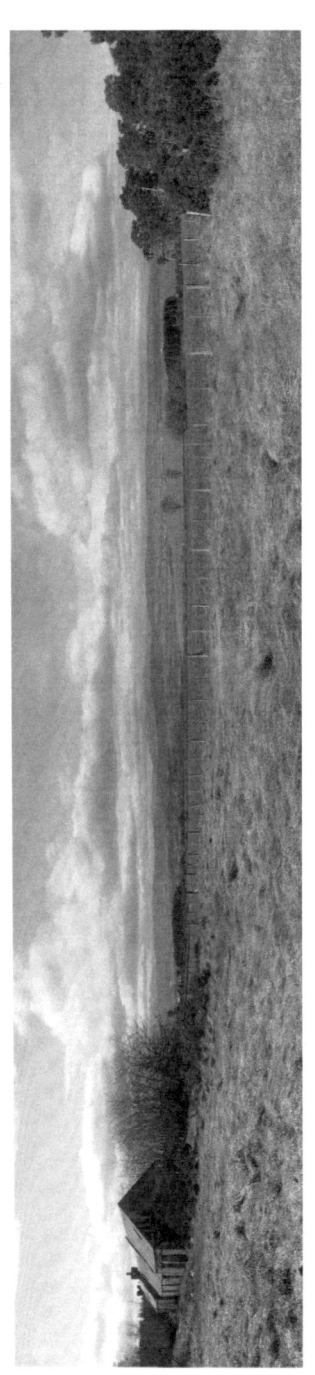

Above: The breathtaking sweep of landscape viewed by Jane Duncan as a child; she did not revisit the abandoned homestead
Below: Both the 1816 plan **(left)** and the first edition of the Ordnance Survey (1870s) show a dotting of small crofts in the district, but by the time of the second edition Ordnance Survey (1907) **(right)** most of these have disappeared leaving only the more substantial *"Colony Mains"*, home of the Camerons.

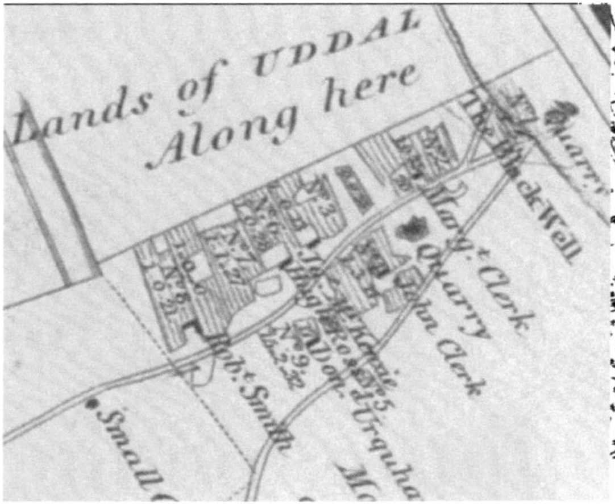

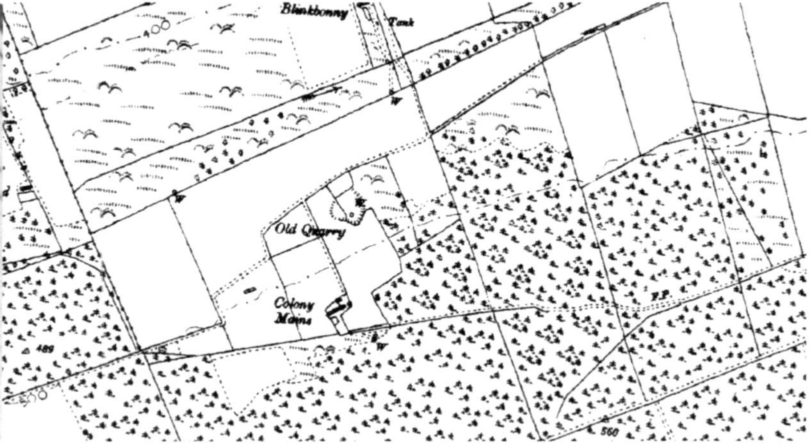

It may be that this settlement was initiated in the moors to support entitlement to part of the Commons (which extended over all the high ground of the Black Isle). Certainly, the detailed plan of the *"Commonty of Milbuy"* drawn up in 1816 to allow division of the Commons amongst the Black Isle estates shows an isolated settlement of 9 small lets closely packed together here in the Commons, hard on the boundary with the Udale Estate, and near the boundary with Poyntzfield. This perhaps suggests the origin of the name *"Colony"* as a *"colonising"* settlement in the moors of the Commons. Curiously, the name itself does not appear frequently in early records — the first occurrence I have noted is in 1834.

In the 1870s, the Ordnance Survey recorded: *"Colony. Authorities for spelling: James Grant Esq farmer Udale by Cromarty, William Hossack crofter Colony by Cromarty, Hugh Munro crofter Colony by Cromarty. This name is applied to a small district situated about five miles to the west of the town of Cromarty comprising small farms or crofts. All the houses in this district are one storey high thatched and in fair repair. Lt. Col. Ross Cromarty House Cromarty Proprietor."*

In a pattern repeated across the Black Isle, small crofts disappeared and the rural population plummeted during the late 1800s-early 1900s, despite new crofting rights. From the Valuation Rolls, there were 11 tenants at the Colony (Cromarty Estate) in 1868-9, but only four in 1900-1 (one being John Cameron, crofter) and only two in 1920-1 (one still part of the Cromarty Estate, the other being John Cameron, now proprietor of his own land). And it was a common occurrence when Duncan Cameron, Jane Duncan's father, felt obliged due to economic circumstances to leave the Colony to go south to join the police in 1899.

Profits improved during both World Wars with stronger demand for home-grown produce, but in the inter-war depression depopulation accelerated, crofts were amalgamated and crofthouses abandoned to fall into the turf. The remaining crofts in the Colony district were amalgamated into the Colony Mains of the Camerons.

With the increase of farm mechanisation post-World War II, ever larger units were found to be more economic. The Camerons held on in the Colony until George was too elderly to keep it up and then, on 23 February 1949, even the Colony was sold (to the Vestey family) and itself amalgamated.

The crofthouse and steading, like Wellhead to the west, are now just empty shells. Inside the crofthouse, there is only air between the fireplaces in the east and west gables. Other ghost steadings like this in the Black Isle have been converted to modern residential uses, but the occasional remote structure like the Colony hangs on as a derelict mockery of the thriving homestead it once was, an unsettling memorial to a lost way of life.

Jemimaville – a guided tour

Jemimaville lies at the eastern extremity of the Parish of Resolis, Udale Burn forming the boundary with the Parish of Cromarty. It was initiated in 1822 by Sir George Gun Munro of Poyntzfield, and named after his wife Jamima Charlotte Graham, daughter of Lieutenant Colonel Colin Dundas Graham of Cromarty House. For many years it was known as *"Jamima Village"* before becoming Jemimaville. For a detailed description of its history, see the Resolis guide.

Jane Duncan, like many other writers, conflates the wives of two different Sir George Gun Munros of Poyntzfield to create a mythical *"Jemima Poyntz"* after whom both Poyntzfield and Jemimaville are named. In *"Letter from Reachfar"* she concludes: *"Miss Jemima Poyntz, if this story is true, and it is fairly well documented, is well commemorated."* In reality, Poyntzfield is named after a Mary Poyntz, whom the first George Gun Munro of Poyntzfield married in 1760, and Jemimaville is named after Jamima Charlotte Graham, whom a later George Gun Munro of Poyntzfield married in 1822.

A scenic spot to park is just to the east of Jemimaville at the observation point of Udale Bay. The plaque here commemorates the role of the Cromarty Firth in war time. The Firth has been home to the British Fleet, including during the wars, and Jane Duncan on several occasions describes the surprising speed with which the big ships would swing around on their buoys on the changing of the tide.

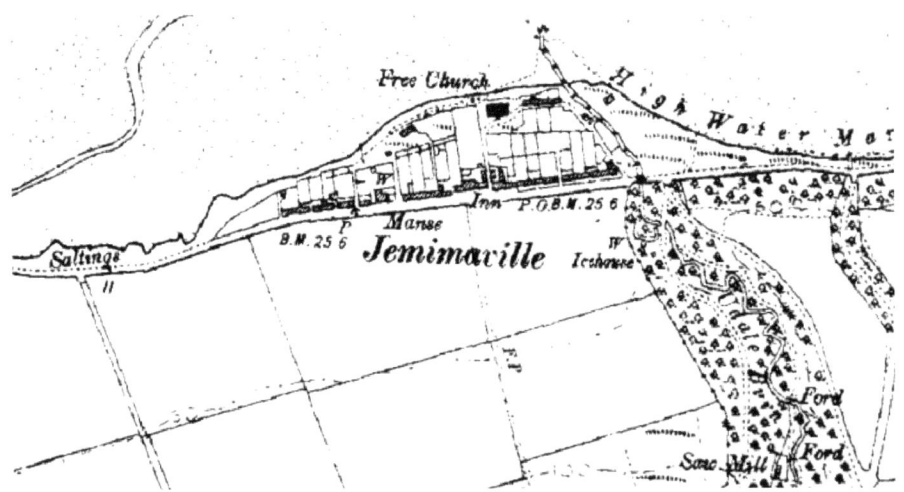

Above: Jemimaville in 1907. Few buildings have been lost or added since that time, but note presence of Sawmill, Icehouse, Inn, Free Church Manse, Free Church and Post Office.

The Black Isle benefited financially from the military presence. Jemimaville, however, suffered in 1914 when, following a false alarm caused by paranoia over suspected submarine activity in the Firth, the village was accidentally shelled. Several houses had roofs holed and a baby, Alexandrina McGill, was seriously injured, although fortunately nobody was killed. The incident was suppressed due to military embarrassment.

Walking west into Jemimaville, we pass the distinctive raised beach that is such a prominent feature of this part of the Black Isle. On it can be seen the line of the uncompleted Cromarty-Dingwall Light Railway, six miles of which were constructed before the first World War. Further into Jemimaville, on the west side of Scott's Garage, the railway bridge over Udale Burn can still be seen.

Scott's Garage (for picture, see Resolis guide) is the first building we come to in Jemimaville and has a surprising history. It was previously the United Free church, erected in 1906 just to the west of Newmills, and re-erected here. Scott's Garage commenced in Jemimaville with a petrol pump in the square and the only taxi in the area. It was the garage owner, Hugh Scott, who conveyed Jane Duncan and his good friend, her Uncle George, from Inverness to Jemimaville on her return to live in the Black Isle in January 1959. The car had to be excavated from a snowdrift and Rose Cottage on arrival was bitterly cold, draughty and without running water.

Above: Jemimaville c 1908; looking east to the Poyntzfield Arms Inn and the Post Office.

On the south side is the impressive stone gateway leading into Udale. The dyke from the gatepiers extends around the former Estate of Udale, running from the burn here up the braes to reach the boundary of the Colony high up on the hill.

In the late 19th century, a sawpit owned by Poyntzfield and containing two circular saws powered by Udale Burn lay on the west side of the burn — the remains can still be seen, a few hundred yards up from the bridge. The Gun Munros at this time owned both Poyntzfield and Udale.

About one hundred yards up from the bridge, built into the west bank, stands a fairly well-preserved icehouse, where ice was stored to keep fish caught in the great stake nets and yairs in Udale Bay fresh whilst being transported by ship to southern markets. The salmon harvested from Udale Bay were of great value to the Poyntzfield Estate, the Newhall Estate (which had its own icehouse at Chapelton Point) and the Cromarty Estate (again with its own icehouse). Indeed, there was a dispute over a contested sea line and stake nets erected off Jemimaville between Sir George Gun Munro of Poyntzfield and the Cromarty Estate in the early 1850s resulting in plans being drawn up which act as a key record of the exact locations of these stake nets and yairs.

Above: Entranceway to the icehouse
Left: Icehouse interior. Ice would have been broken out of frozen ponds on the field behind (to the west) in the winter and shovelled through the hatch near the top.

The heads of families in 1841 were: James Cameron, wright. James Urquhart, fisher. James Ross, mason. John Urquhart, agricultural labourer (ag lab). James McPharquhar, gardener. John McLean, ag lab. William Ross, ag lab. Alexr McKenzie, gardener. Flora McDonald, female servant. Alexr Ross, ag lab. William McKenzie, ag lab. Alexr McKay, ag lab. Hugh Bethune, tailor. Andrew Stewart, ag lab. John McIntosh, tailor. John Urquhart, ag lab. Duncan Munro, ag lab. Widow Munro, female servant. Hugh Sinclair, blacksmith. Mary Ross, female servant. Donald Ross, ag lab. John Campbell, ag lab. Walter Ross, innkeeper (with residents including a quarrier, a wright and a seaman, a Captain White). Hugh Munro, wright. Widow McDonald, female servant. Colin Davidson, tailor. Kenneth Douglas, ag lab. Widow Urquhart, female servant.

There was thus clearly a considerable diversity of tradespeople amongst the mainly farmworking families. This diversity increased as the century progressed.

The first dwelling we come to, having crossed the Udale Burn bridge (which has a datestone of 1800), is the bonny Burnside Cottage (which has a date of 1826 on the marriage lintel).

We come, a short distance along the terrace from Burnside Cottage, to the former village hall, now converted to a house named the Old Hall. Long time residents will remember the Christmas parties here. Jane Duncan came to a deal with James Scott of Scott's Garage regarding this building, exchanging it with a significant sum of money for the ruined old Free Church on the shore. It is thought this was to ensure her ongoing privacy in the Old Store.

Finally, in this first block of buildings in Jemimaville, the most westerly house is a Listed Building, known at time of Listing as Friedlander's House but now called Clarinnis. It lies, like many of the buildings on the street, behind an attractive coped rubble dyke. Like much of Jemimaville it is early to mid 19th century, but with a modern slate roof. It has two delightful cable moulded scrolled skewputts (for photograph, see Resolis guide) and two piended dormer windows.

Clarinnis

Jemimaville contains most of the "C" Listed Buildings in the Parish of Resolis. The old Free Church Manse achieves "B" Listed status. Many folk naturally fret at the constraints that Listing places on the owner and occupier, and there have been some strange decisions on what is acceptable development on such buildings. However, the wonder is that more of the marvellous buildings within Jemimaville have not been given Listed Building status.

All the buildings in the next terrace are Listed, comprising, from east to west, Laurel Cottage, Woodlands, Rosedene, Firthview and, finally, the old Poyntzfield Post Office, now known as Beinn na Meilich.

Listed Buildings from Laurel Cottage west

Laurel Cottage was originally two single storey cottages but with the west one later raised to two storeys. The two cottages now form one house. When Listed, the eastern cottage had a corrugated iron roof but is now slated. Woodlands sits behind a dwarf garden wall with railings and again was raised from its original single storey to two storeys. Rosedene is in a different style again, with *"barge-boarded gablet dormerheads"* at first floor windows, being raised and much altered from its early 19th century origins, and with two attractive canted bay windows. Firthview in pink is dated 1826, again thought to have been elevated to two storeys from an original single storey. The date and initials *"DM"* at the lintel of the door are now obscured by the porch added in 1979. Finally, in this block, is what was Poyntzfield Post Office. Its roof is piended at the west end.

Both the telephone exchange for the area and the Post Office in the village were named Poyntzfield, reflecting the early association with the Estate of Poyntzfield.

Left: The popular Mrs Thomas of the Post Office in Jemimaville c1935

Base, on left: The pump on the east side of the village.
Base, on right: The pump on the west side of the village; this is the one from which the Camerons in Rose Cottage fetched their water.

On the far side of the road from Firthview is one of the two famous pumps of Jemimaville. Residents had to run the gauntlet of traffic to gain their water supply. See the Resolis guide for a poem that celebrated the digging of the two wells and installation of pumps in 1887. The pump here has a plaque with the legend *"Plaque donated by"* but the remainder has been obscured by an application of mortar. When Jane Duncan arrived in Rose Cottage in January 1959, weary and cold, and wishing only for a hot bath, she remembered to her horror that every drop of water had to be carried from the village pump!

There follows to the west another grouping, firstly of the mid-19th century pair of single storey and attic cottages (known at time of Listing as Dale Villa), Barnacle Cottage and Talisker, followed by the substantial Bay View (the former Poyntzfield Arms Inn).

The Poyntzfield Arms was not the only Inn in Jemimaville, for, amazingly for such a small village, in 1861 Jemimaville contained two inns as well as a seller of spirits. But by the 1870s, the Ordnance Survey records simply one, albeit named differently: *"Plough Inn. This names applies to a small one storey thatched Inn with the usual village accommodation. It is situated about the centre of the Village."*

The Resolis guide describes many incidents relating to the lively Poyntzfield Arms Inn. Sadly, like many of the pubs around the Cromarty Firth, the Poyntzfield Arms had its licence bought out and extinguished, on 18 June 1918, as part of the liquor controls around the Firth to protect the forces.

The report for the Central Control Board (Liquor Traffic) reviewing the case for closure noted that *"the business is being carried on by an elderly maiden lady for the behoof of her nephew (a minor) who was commencing his course as a medical student but is presently in the Army."* The lady concerned was Miss May Morrison. The Inn in past years had sold an average of 411.7 proof gallons of spirits and 40 barrels of beer annually. The iron ring outside is understood to be that to which horses were once tethered.

Above: Bay View (the former Poyntzfield Arms Inn) and Listed Buildings to the east

Opposite Bay View, and somewhat surrealistically in a field all by itself, sits the tiny wooden modern Post Office.

The one-sided design of the village, all to the north of the main road, has survived. All attempts to change the physical shape of the village and extend housing into the neighbouring agricultural land have thus far been rejected.

Above: The current village Post Office

Left: Looking across a field, in the days of stooks, to the manse and the Poyntzfield Arms

Below: The village in 2010, still closely bound by fields

The next terrace commences with more Listed Buildings, Trenton and Maryville, again single storey with attic cottages. Adjoining Trenton and Maryville, to the west, is a beautiful but unlisted house, obviously the home of a tailor and built (or altered) somewhat later in 1879 (from the datestone). There are many fascinating architectural features in Jemimaville and here you can see the symbols of the tailor beautifully set out on the wall (for picture, see Resolis guide) and the ornamental skewputts at the bottom of the gable, holding the gable stones in place.

Left: Trenton and Maryville, and the east skewputt of the tailor's building

The aim of the laird of Poyntzfield, Sir George Gun Munro, in creating Jemimaville was to create a modern working village populated with not only agricultural labourers but also tradesmen and artisans. Thus he was advertising in the newspapers from the 1820s for craftsmen and tradesmen to move into the area. The Inverness Courier carried advertisements such as: 1826 *"FEUS in Jamemaville on very advantageous terms; also very profitable situations for Tailors and Shoemakers, who can command a little Capital..."* Later in 1826: *"A very eligible situation for a good Shoemaker at Jamemaville."*

He was also creating and developing industry and markets. In 1833 he was advertising: *"Notice. New markets at Jamima Village .. Three Markets, for the sale of horses, cattle Pigs Farm and every kind of produce."*

And in 1841, there were great celebrations for the launch of the first ship (a barque of 80 tons), built in the new ship building yard at Jemimaville. In the front of a great crowd, the Proprietor's wife, Mrs Jemima Munro, launched the ship, breaking a bottle of wine on the bowsprit, and naming it — the Jemima.

The village was named after Jemima Charlotte Graham, daughter of Lieutenant Colonel Colin Dundas Graham of Cromarty House and Mary de Jenatsch.

Her first husband was Francis Graham, a sugar plantation attorney in Jamaica, who owned a sugar estate in Jamaica called Tulloch. (The Grahams and the Davidsons of Tulloch at Dingwall were closely tied financially). Sadly their children died in Jamaica and Francis himself died quite young. Shortly after his death in Jamaica in 1820, Jamima Charlotte Graham returned to Britain.

In 1822 she married the then Major George Gun Munro of Poyntzfield, Black Isle, at Richmond, Surrey, and it is noted from official records entitled *"Returns of Slaves"* that in turn he became owner of the Tulloch estate, St Thomas in the Vale, Jamaica. Jemimaville thus has roots in sugar and slavery.

Similarly, the first husband, George Hinde, of Mary Poyntz (wife of the first George Gun Munro of Poyntzfield), the agent of Boyds in Jamaica, died young in Jamaica. In a letter written in 1756 about his business affairs we read: *"we are sorry to hear Mr. Hinde is dead. He stood your Climate but a very little while (poor Gentleman)."* There was money to be made in the West Indies, if you survived.

Jemima died at Poyntzfield House aged 72 in 1867.

The final building in this block is the delightful Rose Cottage, into which Jane Duncan moved in 1959. We shall come back to this key point, but for now will pass on to the next building, the separate and substantial former Free Church manse (for picture, see Resolis guide).

The manse is one of the most striking buildings you note as you pass through Jemimaville, its unusual design including bowed outer bays linked above the front door by a piended roof supported by two columns. This was the home of the famous Reverend Donald Sage, author of an enjoyable book of parish life in the 19th century called *"Memorabilia Domestica"*. He left the established church in 1843 with most of his congregation to join the newly-formed Free Church during the great Disruption.

A series of Free Church ministers, including Donald Sage, James McLauchlan and John McIver, and a series of local doctors, including Dr Richard Dick, Dr Lewis Lawson and Dr Thomas Homer, lived in the manse. It is currently being renovated.

It was through Jemimaville on 29 September 1843 that a mob of irate Resolis citizens marched on their way to the Cromarty Courthouse. They were bound to rescue an old lady who had been seized as one of the rioters at Resolis Church the day before. The evidence of John Urquhart, a quarrier at Cullicudden, and one of the witnesses at the subsequent trial in Edinburgh, describes the events as well as recording the two new Free Churches being built at Jemimaville and Cromarty.

He states *"that there had been a riot and disturbance that day at the Church of Resolis, and that a woman of the name of Margaret Cameron had been taken to the Gaol of Cromarty. That the Declarant had occasion to go to Cromarty the next day to see Thomas Murray the Contractor for the Free Church there, about the dimensions of some stones which were wanted by him. That he and his brother Donald Urquhart left Cullicudden early in the forenoon of that day, to go to Cromarty. That when they had got as far as the Church of Resolis, about two miles from Cullicudden, they fell in with a Crowd of people, the greater part of whom were women. That he and his brother remained there upwards of half an hour, and heard some of them say that they intended to go to Cromarty and get Margaret Cameron out of Prison, but he cannot recollect any particular person who said so. That his brother and he accompanied by a good many of the Crowd proceeded towards Cromarty as far as Jamimaville, when the Declarant parted from his brother and the Crowd and went down to look at the new Church, where he remained about a quarter of an hour. That on proceeding to Cromarty, Declarant found the Crowd had got there before him..."*

The Gaol was stormed and Margaret Cameron rescued, but the disturbances brought out the military and the supposed ringleaders were eventually convicted. The sentences they received were relatively light for the time, perhaps so as to not to encourage further trouble.

A short distance west of the former manse is an imposing red sandstone two and a half storey block with projecting skewputts which contained the grocery store run by the well-liked James and Kathy Ferguson. James was a representative of the family of Fergusons who have lived in the neighbouring farm of Ardoch for over 150 years.

Right: Former grocery store, Jemimaville

Isabella Ferguson, of the Ardoch family, married Jane Duncan's Uncle George in 1915. Tragically, she died at Ardoch shortly after her one-day old child died in 1917 and she is buried in Kirkmichael (her husband is buried in Cromarty).

Passing the second of the village pumps, we reach the final block of Listed Buildings comprising, from east to west, Langlands Cottage and Red Rock Cottage. Langlands Cottage is one of the few buildings in Jemimaville still to retain the once-common corrugated iron roof. Red Rock Cottage was known at time of Listing as Drought's Cottage. Both of these are mid nineteenth century single storey and attic cottages. They have rubble walls with dressed margins.

Above right:
Langlands Cottage and Red Rock Cottage
*c*1920

Below right:
The same buildings in 2010; identical save for the dormers on Langlands

The former Church of Scotland Mission is to the south of the road. Leaving Jemimaville, we come to the RSPB hide. From here, a host of birds all year round may be observed, including vast numbers of migratory and wintering wildfowl and waders. Nigg and Udale Bays comprise a National Nature Reserve, and there is an RSPB leaflet for the site. If we were to continue around Udale Bay we would come to Kirkmichael, the final destination of many Jemimaville residents.

Rose Cottage and the Old Store

But let us now return to Rose Cottage, where Jane Duncan first lived when she moved back to the Highlands, to dwell in Jemimaville. As we pause in front of Rose Cottage, this is our opportunity to review the story of Jane Duncan in the area.

John Cameron, the crofter of the Colony, had two sons. One was Duncan (Jane Duncan's father) and the other was George (her Uncle George). Duncan moved south to join the police, working his way up to Police Sergeant. George stayed on at the Colony. Duncan married Jessie Sandison, daughter of a traction engine driver, in 1909. Elizabeth Jane Cameron was born in Dunbartonshire in 1910 and attended Lenzie Academy and Glasgow University but spent her holidays in her blessed Colony. She would be sent home to the Colony with a label bearing her name and address pinned inside the coat and her Uncle George would pick her up at Inverness, cross the station platform and board the little Black Isle train that would take them to Fortrose where the horse and trap were stabled. Her brother Jock (1919-1973) was also born in the south, but when their mother died in 1921, Jock was sent back to his grandparents in the Colony.

Her father re-married in 1925, his second wife being his housekeeper, Christina Maitland. Jane Duncan found her Aberdonian stepmother difficult to live with, and relished her trips to the Colony. She says she was not a clever child but despite this became the Dux of Lenzie Academy and enrolled as a student at Glasgow University. When she graduated with her MA in English she returned to the Colony and seemed prepared to settle there indefinitely, but felt it was expected of her to do something more with her expensive education than domestic duties on the farm.

It was difficult in the depression between wars to find a suitable job, but she tried her hand as a governess, companion, secretary and even a model. During World War II she worked in Photographic Intelligence which was more fulfilling. She then became a secretary in an engineering company where she met Sandy Clapperton. Her heroine, Janet Sandison, in her *"Friends"* series, becomes a secretary in an engineering company and marries an Alexander Alexander, whom she calls *"Twice"* because of his name. All through her writing are these strange parallels.

In real life, Sandy was separated from his Roman Catholic wife whom he could not divorce. However, he and Elizabeth Jane set up home in Jamaica in 1949, where Sandy was chief engineer on a sugar plantation. When he fell ill, she took one of her many manuscripts out of the linen cupboard and sent it to an agent, who hawked it around until it was picked up (indirectly through the recommendation of a reader) by Macmillans. This was *"My Friend Muriel"*.

After discovering this was but one of seven books in the series, Macmillans accepted them all, but decided to publish "*My Friends the Miss Boyds*" first as it was chronologically at the beginning of the story of Janet Sandison.

Sandy died in 1958 and she returned to Britain. Having sorted her affairs out with her publishers, she returned to the north on a bleak January evening in 1959. She was met off the train by her Uncle George and his friend Hugh Scott of the garage in Jemimaville. As the Colony had been sold, she was moving in with her Uncle George in Rose Cottage.

Above: Rose Cottage, with the Old Store behind

George had sole occupation of Rose Cottage by now. Her grandfather had died at the Colony in 1934 and at that time her retired Police Sergeant father Duncan was already living in Rose Cottage with his second wife, "*Kirsty*". When George could no longer manage the Colony and it was sold in 1949, he moved down from the hill to live with them. Duncan died in 1951 and Kirsty moved out to live with a sister, and so on Jane Duncan's return it was just she and her Uncle together.

My great grandparents, George Munro and Annie Grant McCaskill, lived in Rose Cottage immediately before Jane Duncan's father. It was purchased on 18 September 1930 for £65 from George Munro, who had moved out to live with his son-in-law, James Young Ferguson, in Auchmartin. It points up another Cameron connection with their Colony neighbours, the Fergusons of Ardoch, as James Young Ferguson himself was from Ardoch.

That first night back in Rose Cottage, Jane Duncan told her Uncle for the first time she had written a book but confessed she didn't know if her writing would pay. He offered to keep them afloat adding *"You keep going at the books."*

But her writing was successful from the outset, with My Friends the Miss Boyds becoming a bestseller. During the 1960s and 1970s Jane Duncan wrote a book a year, writing in a burst between January and March. And as her books continued to sell worldwide, she could buy and restore the ruined *"Old Store"* on the shore of Udale Bay, just below the Rose Cottage garden. She and her Uncle moved there, leaving the cottage free for visitors and members of the family.

The Old Store is similar to *"girnals"* around the Cromarty Firth, storehouses on the shore where grain from estate tenants paid as rent would be measured, stored and shipped out to southern markets. John Ferguson, farmer at Ardoch, bought it from one of the Gun Munros of Poyntzfield and it was used simply as an implement shed for the Fergusons of Ardoch and Auchmartin. Jane Duncan purchased it in 1961 from the Fergusons (yet another connection with the Fergusons of Ardoch!) and converted it to the home in which she would spend the remainder of her life.

Above: A delightful picture of a smiling Jane Duncan in front of her as-yet unconverted Old Store

A path comes down beside the garden of Rose Cottage and in front of the Old Store, but Jane Duncan and visitors used the gate at the bottom of the Rose Cottage garden to cross the few feet between the two gardens. Jane Duncan in *"Letter from Reachfar"* tells a great story of when she loans Rose Cottage to a Professor of English Literature who holds a dinner party in the cottage. In the party is author Neil Gunn, who asks for gin, a drink the Professor and his wife do not have in stock. However, their children know of a secret supply in the privet hedge outside Rose Cottage. Her kind neighbour who trims the hedges for her did not *"drink"* while working but always kept an odd bottle of gin or two in the hedges, in the apple trees and in his hen-house — in case he became thirsty.

She remained in the Old Store for the remainder of her life, until she died of a heart attack there in 1976, aged 66. Her death certificate curiously gives her name as Clapperton, although she and Sandy had never married. She is buried in Kirkmichael, within sight of both the Colony and her two homes in Jemimaville.

Close to the Old Store (now also called *"Reachfar"*) is the site of the first school in Jemimaville. The Reverend Donald Sage was successful in gaining approval in 1826 for a school in the new village. The school and schoolmaster's house were built and kept in repair largely by Sir George Gun Munro of Poyntzfield himself.

Not far east of the Old Store is another site she purchased, the first Resolis Free Church (see Resolis guide for picture). She probably obtained the ruin to protect her privacy. It may be that privacy was also one of the reasons for her opening her *"Friendly Shop"* in Cromarty, selling teas and offering an opportunity where she could meet fans of her *"Friendly"* series and the public well away from her home.

The first Resolis Free Church was originally built here in 1843 after the Disruption simply because it was the only place made available for it, given the general hostility of the landowners, with one exception. The Records of 15 August 1843 state: *"The Committee met this day in the Schoolhouse [Jemimaville], for the purpose of contracting the building of a Free Church at Jamimaville on the site granted by Sir George Gunn Munro of Poyntzfield."* The congregation was reluctant about constructing it here on the extreme east end of the Parish of Resolis, but nevertheless a very solid and imposing building was raised. The location was never popular, though, so when the opportunity came up for a central location in 1867, it was seized upon and both a new Church and a new Manse were erected there.

From the ruins of the church, one corner of which is now close to being washed away by the sea, it is a short walk back past the Railway Bridge to return to the Udale Bay observation point to the east of Jemimaville where our tour commenced.

The Cameron Family

Although associated with Newton and the Colony for a long time, nevertheless the first record of the Cameron family shows an origin in the Parish of Resolis rather than the Parish of Cromarty. Jane Duncan's great grandfather, Donald Cameron or McKeddie, was born in **Resolis**, according to his Census returns, to a George Cameron and Jane Urquhart, according to his death certificate. At some point they moved to Cromarty as, when Donald married Janet Grant in 1818, they were *"both at Nielstown"*. Donald lived as an agricultural labourer, road contractor and crofter in Neilston and Newton until he died in 1891.

Family historians will be aware that the dates of the same events can vary depending on source and the Camerons' records demonstrate this. Similarly, surnames were less fixed in the 1700s-1800s, with many families going by an *"alias"* or *"patronymic."* In both parishes of Cromarty and Resolis, McKeddie was a common alias for Cameron, and was used sometimes by officials against the inclination of the family. In Resolis, Christian Cameron in 1834 successfully obtained a formal amendment to the 1796 Resolis baptism register. She protested that: *"the real surname of her & of her brother's family and forefathers is Cameron, but that from the first of them who came to reside in this Country they Received the patronimick Surname of Mackiddy."* Jane Duncan's family similarly answered to both Cameron and McKeddie in the various records.

The age and, by inference, birth year, of that first well-recorded family member, Donald Cameron or McKeddie, depending on source, are thus challenging: death certificate in 1891 - 97 (1794), gravestone in 1891 - 98 (1793), census 1891 - 96 (1795), census 1881 - 80 (1801), census 1871 - 72 (1799), census 1861 - 62 (1799), census 1851 - 54 (1797), census 1841 (where ages were rounded) - 40 (1801). We thus have a birth year for Donald in the period 1793-1801. His death certificate says his parents were George Cameron and Jane Urquhart. Now, there is a Donald born in 1797 to a George McKeddie, weaver in Resolis, and an Isobel Urquhart, but unless either his death certificate or the baptism register incorrectly recorded his mother's Christian name, this may be a red herring.

His son John Cameron (born *c*1846), Jane Duncan's grandfather, worked on several farms in Ross and Cromarty. He married Catherine McRae or Campbell in Knockbain in 1875. From various sources we see him as a farm servant (1861, Newton), agricultural labourer (1871, Allangrange Mains, Knockbain), ploughman (1875, Allangrange), grieve (1878, at Achilty, Contin), cattleman (1879, 1881, 1883, Cromarty Mains), and farm manager (1885, Woodside, Cromarty), until he settled as a crofter in the Colony in 1889 as a tenant in his own right.

Much of the subsequent Cameron history can be summarised from a handful of headstones in the graveyards in Cromarty and Kirkmichael. The Cameron family plot in Cromarty is bounded by four marker stones, each bearing "*DC*" for Donald Cameron. There are two stones.

One stone commemorates Jane Duncan's great grandparents. It is a worn, red sandstone headstone, with a curved top, inscribed: "Erected / by / DONALD CAMERON / in memory of his spouse / JANET GRANT / who died the 16 October / 1849 / aged 52 years / Also / DONALD CAMERON / who died at Newton / 9 May 1891 aged 98 years / Deeply regretted by all who knew him."

The second commemorates Jane Duncan's grandparents, her father, his second wife (but not his first) and her Uncle George. It is a substantial obelisk, surmounted by urn, with the inscription: "Erected by / JOHN CAMERON / in memory of / his sister BELLA / who died at Newton 8th May 1898, / aged 65 years. / Also his daughter / JESSIE, / who died at / the Colony, / 13th May 1911, / aged 30 years. / And his daughter / MARJORY, / died 10th June 1916, / aged 24 years. / Also the above / JOHN CAMERON, / died 8th May 1934 / aged 91 years. / [on pedestal] And of his wife / CATHERINE CAMPBELL, / died 17th June 1934 / aged 81 years. / [on side of obelisk] Also / in memory of / his son / DUNCAN CAMERON / died 16th December 1951 / aged 73 years. / Also his beloved wife / CHRISTINA MAITLAND / died 24th August 1959 / aged 74 years. / Also / GEORGE CAMERON / brother of DUNCAN / died 19th March 1968 / aged 88 years."

In Kirkmichael, a lonely grey granite headstone, with a curved top, commemorates Isabella Ferguson, the young wife of Jane Duncan's Uncle George, who died tragically early following the birth of their first child who died one day old. It bears the inscription: "In / loving memory of / ISABELLA FERGUSON, / died at Ardoch, 23rd May 1917. / Beloved wife of / GEORGE CAMERON." It is a fairly substantial stone, with no others nearby. It is suprising that her husband is not buried beside her and that his death is not commemorated on her stone rather than being tacked onto his brother's inscription in Cromarty.

In Kirkmichael, Jane Duncan's stone, a grey granite headstone, with a flat top, simply says: "In / memory of / JANE DUNCAN / (ELIZABETH JANE CAMERON) / author / died 20th October 1976 / aged 66 years".

For the latter day Camerons, Jane Duncan's nephews and niece, who still return to Rose Cottage nowadays, just as they did when visiting their aunt, the reader is referred to the centenary booklet on Jane Duncan and the appendix to the new edition of "*My Friends the Miss Boyds*". Their father and mother are buried in Kirkmichael — the headstone stands just behind that of Jane Duncan.

Published in Great Britain, 2010, by:

Jim Mackay
Firichean House
Cullicudden
Dingwall
Scotland IV7 8LL

The moral right of the author has been asserted.

All rights reserved. No part of this publication may be reproduced, stored in a retrieval system, or transmitted, in any form or by any means, electronic, mechanical, photocopying, recording or otherwise, without the express prior permission of the publisher given in writing.

British Library Cataloguing-in-Publication Data
A catalogue record for this book is available from the British Library.

ISBN 978-0-9562102-1-0

Typeset by Jim Mackay.

Profits from sales will go to the Kirkmichael Trust, which seeks to restore the Kirkmichael site in Resolis for public benefit; for information see the Trust's website:
www.kirkmichael.info

Text copyright © 2010 by James Murdoch Mackay